A Collec

SPLATTERS OF THE HEART

Simone C. Phillips, LMSW

WRITERS REPUBLIC L.L.C.

515 Summit Ave. Unit R1
Union City, NJ 07087, USA

Website: *www.writersrepublic.com*
Hotline: *1-877-656-6838*
Email: *info@writersrepublic.com*

Ordering Information:
Quantity sales. Special discounts are available on quantity purchases by corporations, associations, and others. For details, contact the publisher at the address above.

Library of Congress Control Number: 2021915316
ISBN-13: 978-1-63728-526-8 [Paperback Edition]
978-1-63728-527-5 [Digital Edition]

Rev. date: 11/16/2021

"Simone has great academic abilities including an ability to use writing to express great feeling and sensitivity. She is one of the most talented second grade writers that I have ever taught."

MR. DAVID GRIST
FORMER SECOND GRADE TEACHER
EXCERPT FROM SECOND GRADE PROGRESS REPORT
ELMHURST ELEMENTARY SCHOOL
1995-1996

DEDICATION

This book is dedicated to my "Wetta," also known as, mom. Ever since I was little you told me to publish my poems. Thank you for giving me stability as a child so I could achieve the highest tier on Maslow's Hierarchy of Needs model. Las Vegas has been a bumpy ride, but together we've pulled through and regained stability. You get on my nerves sometimes, but life wouldn't be the same without you! I love you!

DEDICATION

To my Sister, Cousin, Friend (Leelee),
Our daily check-in's have been the highlight of my life for the past 7 years! God knew I needed you and I'm never letting go! Thank you for being you! I love you!

To my Gran Gran,
Thank you for being so strong! Your strength amazes me! Thank you for giving our family stability. I know it wasn't easy, but it paid off! I love you!

To my dad,
Thank you for your emotional support and for always making me laugh. You always make me crack a smile even when I don't want to. I love you!

To Cydni Chanae,
Thank you for being such a great friend for the past 14 years. You really showed me what a good friend is! Love you long time!

A SPECIAL THANK YOU

To Ebony Rose,
Thank you for the bravery you possessed to tell your story. Because of your courage, I gained the strength to tell mine. Your legacy will live on forever.

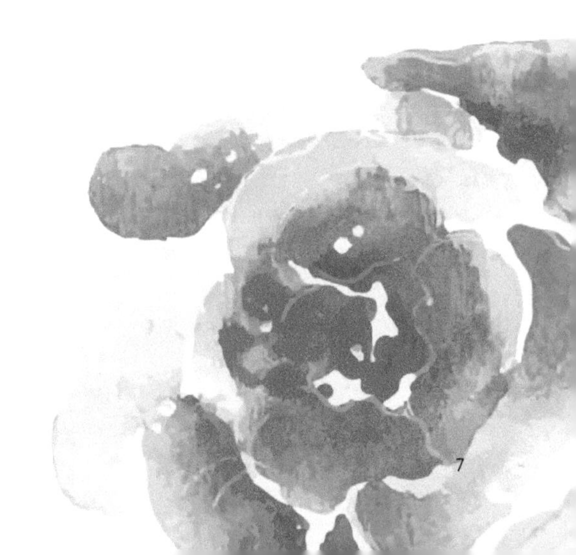

TABLE OF CONTENTS

TABLE OF
CONTENTS

ABOUT THE AUTHOR

Simone Phillips is a licensed master social worker in the state of Nevada. She obtained her undergraduate degree in Early Childhood Education from the University of Las Vegas, Nevada in May 2014 and her Master of Social Work degree from Simmons University in May 2018.

Simone was born and raised in Lansing, MI. At the age of 19, she moved to Las Vegas, Nevada in hopes to see a "great move of God," as her former pastor preached. Over the course of eight years in Las Vegas, Simone began to realize that her church lacked integrity and operated like a cult.

During her time of disillusionment, Simone used writing poetry as a healthy coping mechanism. Now, after six years of leaving the cult-like entity, she decided to publish 33 poems for her 33rd birthday. Some of the poems highlight her feelings of confusion and bewilderment, while others are about love.

For more information about her experience, check out her YouTube channel entitled, The Disillusioned Church Girl. There is a QR code and link located on the last page of this book.

Splatters of the Heart was originally inspired by a local poetry contest in March 2021. Simone entered 10 poems into the contest; however, none of her poems were selected. Since Simone lives by the mantra "rejection is redirection," she gathered more poems and decided to publish them in hopes to share her experiences through poetry on a larger platform.

Simone loves writing poetry and has used her gift to get through some of her toughest obstacles and greatest losses. Some of her plans include creating affordable housing and a hotel for individuals suffering from homelessness. She desires to provide services in such a capacity that everyone can have the basic necessities to achieve the top tier on Maslow's Hierarchy of Needs model.

ACKNOWLEDGEMENTS

I would first like to thank God. Even though I am still confused about a lot of things, I still believe that there is a deity that made the earth so beautiful and so amazing. I can't help but look at all the beautiful creations and not think about a creator too. So, thank you God for this opportunity.

I want to thank Sonya Shaffner (Mama Shaff) for literally being my unofficial godmother! Thank you for spoiling me with love, kindness, and attention ever since I was 11 years old. Thank you for literally being the village that my mom needed to help raise me. You gave me safety, comfort, and stability and you've always exceeded my expectations of what love is! I am so grateful for you and I love you so much! I can't wait to bless you the way you've always gone out of your way to bless me.

I want to thank my Aunt Ree Ree, Aunt Cherie, Aunt Sonya, Aunt Shonee, Aunt Stacy, Auntie Beverly, Aunt Cindy, Aunt Marcia, and Aunt Angie for loving me so much and spoiling me rotten! Though you guys are miles away, I always felt your love! Aunties are the best! I'm so glad God created aunties! LOL!

I would like to thank my uncles (Shelton, Erwin, Lawrence, Odell and Randall) for being men of integrity and not abusing me, but rather being that added support to fill in my dad's shoes when needed. You guys all gave me space to develop and mature so I could reach my full potential and I LOVE YOU so much for that! You all have a special place in my heart.

I would like to thank a special person who was very pivotal in helping me process my hurt and anxiety after leaving my former church. Thank you for all the lunch dates and family gatherings that you've consistently invited me to even though I always declined to come (LOL). Thank you for displaying strength after you left the "church" because it really gave me the strength to leave too. I love you and I'm so grateful to have you in my life.

I would like to thank Danielle Radford for creating a bond with me when I was 19 years old and never letting it break. She has celebrated me every single year on my birthday and has showered me with kindness though she is thousands of miles away! I love you Chica!

ACKNOWLEDGEMENTS

I would like to thank my former coworker and marketing manager Tomecia Allen. Thank you for helping me manifest my dreams and make them tangible! I really appreciate the time and energy that you have invested in me! Love you girl!

I would like to thank TLP for being a consistent therapeutic component in my life. Thank you for our quarterly therapy sessions that have pushed me to set boundaries, love myself, and not fall prey to narcissists (LOL). Your comedic relief is very refreshing as well! I love and appreciate you!

To my superstar cousin Marian Jean Derrico. Words cannot express how much I value our relationship! I'm so grateful for our talks and girls nights. Your wisdom is so vast and helpful! I pray God gives you many more years because you're my buddy!

I would like to thank all of my cousins for loving me and always making me feel special, especially Thomas Alexander and Aaron Alexander. I always need an inhaler due to laughing so much around you. Thank you both for going beyond the call of duty of a cousin and stepping into the big brother realm. I love you guys!

I would like to thank my seeestah, Dr. Crystal Allen, all the way from Zemunda and Wakanda! Thank you for being such a ray of sunshine on the first day of my internship for my master's program. I knew I would get a master's degree in the end, but I didn't know I would get a lifelong sister and friend too! Thank you for your light, your love, and your energy! And thank you for being the first person to invest in this book! I love you with my whole heart!

I would like to thank my godmother Katrina Scott, my godsisters Katrina Jackson and Kyla Lily, and my godbrother Isaac Calvin Vinson. Auntie Trina (godmom), Thank you for babysitting me for several years, making me laugh, and telling me I'm beautiful every day. Little Trina, thank you for being such a good example of black excellence! I admire all of your accomplishments and you're an amazing mom! Isaac and Kyla, I love you both so much and I'm proud of you!

ACKNOWLEDGEMENTS

I would like to thank my other mama, Mama Esther McClain for always making me feel extra special at church. Thank you for treating me like your own daughters and not disowning me when I ate all your cashews LOL. Thank you also for entrusting me with your puppies and giving me the opportunity to have my first puppy best friends, Quincy and Zoe. I love you so much!

I would like to thank Christina Pamela (Stinky), for being a consistent friend and sister for the last 23 years. You were the first person to randomly text me during the toughest week of my life and ask me if I wanted to go get a foot massage (LOL). You'll always have a special place in my heart and I'll only ride on the hood of cars in my pajamas with you! LOL!

I would like to thank Tamara Muldrew (TamFam) and Dante Tucker (Tayter Tot) for being my consistent family while here in Las Vegas. TamFam thank you for your love, your guidance, your hugs and for letting me come over your house almost every week. Your home was an outlet for me when I was in a really dark place. Thank you so much! Tayter Tot, I love you and I'm so proud of who you are.

I would like to thank the illustrious, Ms. Amanda Gorman, the youngest inaugural poet, for reviving poetry and reminding the world how powerful and moving words are with just one poem. Watching you read your poem at President Biden's inauguration reignited the gift inside of me to write. Thank you for your bravery, class, and grace that you embodied while reading your poem. You are the epitome of Black Girl Magic.

I want to thank the Canva app for making my creative ideas for this book come to life! I made almost everything from my phone! You guys are amazing!

I want to thank Grammarly for checking all of my editing mistakes and taking away my grammar phobia while putting this project together (LOL).

Lastly, I want to thank you, the reader, for purchasing my book! Thank you for your time as you get a glimpse of the splatters of my heart. Always remember that sometimes life feels like spilled paint, but when it spills on a canvas, it's art!

With love, Simone

AWKWARD ACKNOWLEDGEMENTS

To my former "church" family. I feel super awkward writing this, but I don't care because I really love ya'll! I have so many fun memories with you guys! I know you are forbidden to talk to me, but just know that I think about all of you often and laugh at the good times we had to this day.

To my big sister and church decor leader, I'm so glad you gifted me that afghan back in Michigan because it created an inseparable bond. I know we haven't talked in almost 7 years, but you still mean so much to me! Thank you for loving me while I was at church. I felt so alone, but not with you!

To my favorite little sister who still checks on me to this day! If people could be more like you, the world would be such an amazing place! You are beautiful inside and out and I love you and your mom and dad (PLINK) so much!

To the deacon that always bowed humbly as he opened the door for the church members and told me "You're a precious young lady." You always made me feel special to the point where I thought, "Maybe I really am special." You said it every time you saw me ever since I was 10 years old. Thank you for the weekly affirmations for almost 15 years.

To my favorite big sister in 9th grade. You were a senior and you spoiled me by taking me to lunch in your mom's silver Jeep Liberty until you got your own "YAMAHA" (LOL). I know our closeness dissipated in Vegas, but this book is totally inspired by our poetry book that we tragically lost. You taught me to use poetry to cope at a young age! The only poem I remember was entitled Eve, (LOL). I love you forever, no matter what!

To the male usher that gave me the nickname "Testimony Simoney." There was never a time I saw you that you didn't make me smile! Thank you and your wife for always loving me and making me feel special (The Godiva Chocolate Family).

AWKWARD ACKNOWLEDGEMENTS

To my neighbor (big sister) who is yet teaching me how to stand up for myself! I think my most favorite memory of you is when you wanted to "run up" to that lady's house to get two weeks worth of babysitting money that I was cheated out of. LOL! Thank you for checking on me throughout the years to make sure I was ok! I love you and I appreciate you!

To my FAV and his beautiful wife! Thanks for chatting with me about careers! I got my master's degree in social work like we discussed and now I'm pursuing my clinical license. I remember you told me that clinical social workers make more money. Thank you for your guidance and your high fives! Thank you to your wife for being the best choir partner ever! I always had a blast standing next to her (Lord we praise you!) LOL!

To the male usher that randomly sat down with me and told me that I should pick a career that will generate enough revenue to pay off my student loans. You were right LOL! I appreciate your time then and also when you talked with me outside of Raising Cane's after I left the church to encourage me to come back.

To the praise team leader and her daughter that allowed me to live with them in Summerlin for $300 a month. This really meant a lot to me and made it easier for me to participate in Prima's activities, when she allowed me to come. You both are on my "return the blessing" list. Suga, thank you for always giving me cute clothes.

To the tall and stately church member that gives the most passionate and loving hugs! Thank you for always loving me and making me feel special! I still have the ring you gave me.

To the minster with the cute dog named Frosty. I love you so much! You've always been such a beam of light and you always made me feel loved and special. I appreciate you so much!

With love, Simone

AWKWARD ACKNOWLEDGEMENTS

Clears throat and grabs some water To Prima....You were totally my favorite person! I was always grateful for my skin tone because it was similar to yours! As a senior in high school, instead of researching what career field to go into, I was hoping and praying I could be your armor bearer, your side kick and your kick stand (LOL)! I wanted to be there for you whenever you needed anything, but oftentimes I was rejected by you.

So thank you Prima! Thank you for the rejection! I appreciate the handful of positive moments we shared, but I am so grateful for the rejection. If you hadn't rejected me time and time again, I wouldn't be publishing this book and I wouldn't be getting ready to change Las Vegas and then the world after that!

Thank you for every NO! Thank you for not letting me come to your house because I bought my own house and now I'm working on housing those suffering from homelessness. Thank you for every time you left me out, because now I pay attention to those who are left out of society and get ideas to help meet their needs. Thank you for every tear of disillusionment that I shed as a result of my interactions with you. And thank you for refusing to let me participate in the YouTube project just because I went to go celebrate my grandmother's 75th birthday. I have my own YouTube channel now.

Thank you for every lie of manipulation that you told me in order for me to give my hard-earned money for trips I could not afford. I will be getting every dime back with this book you are reading now. Thank you again so much for your rejection because it was God's way of selecting me to do something bigger and greater than I could have possibly thought of at that time. Below is an excerpt from Bishop T.D. Jakes that confirms why I am so grateful for your rejection.

"[God] predestined an environment that would cause [me] to be rejected out of several places so that [I] would not rest beneath [my] destiny. He disrupted [my] circumstances. He moved [my] life around. He ordered [my] steps. He determined who [I] hooked up [with]. He determined the level of [my] rejection. He prescribed the level and intensity of [my] pain so [I] would have enough conviction when [I] got up to be forceful about this. He pulled [me] backwards far enough so [I] would shoot forward far enough on the basis of this foreknowledge." —Bishop T.D. Jakes (excerpt from the message "Called").

So, thank you so much "dear", as your mom would say. Your rejection has catapulted me into greatness!

Bless You Dear,

Simone

AWKWARD ACKNOWLEDGEMENTS

Clears throat, grabs water and inhaler To Giovanni... I always thought you would reach out so we could have one last chat and make amends. I imagined you saying something like, "Mone, I had small pockets of time to reflect on the events that occurred between us and I want you to know that I apologize for not being honest with you. I know we aren't close anymore, but I'm glad to see you're still fulfilling the success story I prayed about during your associate degree celebration dinner. Kind Regards, Giovanni."

In exchange for my fantasy chat, I think I got subliminal signals from you wishing my existence was erased (LOL), but if you ever decide to accept the fact that I am still in the land of the living and wonder why I put my story on blast, it's for two reasons. Number 1: I'm "giving God something to work with," as you coined the phrase. I'm giving God my bottled-up tears in the form of a poetry book to create revenue to fulfill my dreams. Number two: To date, I have never felt so attached to anyone in my life outside of my immediate family than you. You have no idea the excitement and joy that you brought to my life and to lose that was utterly devastating. I actually count it as one of my greatest losses. I had never experienced a significant loss before losing you, and just like losing a deceased loved one, the void never goes away. With that being said, this book is to help cope with my loss.

It's been seven years since we last talked and I always felt like there wasn't any closure. I always thought you'd reach out, but you didn't. So, here is my closure: Thank you for giving me the opportunity to love unequivocally. Maybe what I was feeling wasn't love, but whatever it was, it was an ethereal experience.

Thanks for being consistent and for pushing me towards education. When I got my master's degree, I thought to myself, "Giovanni would've been so proud of me." You have a gift that makes everyone you come in contact with feel individually special. Don't be ashamed of that. You have a lot to offer this world and you made a huge positive impact on my life. Thank you for being the bank that didn't charge interest (LOL) and thank you for allowing me to talk to you about anything without judgment. You really meant a lot to me.

Kind Regards,
Simone

Green

Green is mean,
It flows down a stream.
It makes me want to make it beam.

It's green you,
Do you know what to do?

So if you see a beam of green,
Stay back you might scream,

Because it's mean!

*First poem ever written
Elmhurst Elementary
1997 Newsletter (3rd Grade)

Deflection

Projection,
Deflection,
You're going in the wrong direction.

You continue to point and blame,
But I'm not the cause of your pain.

Objection,
Correction,
You could use some introspection.

Look deep down inside,
What are those feelings you're trying to hide?

Detection,
Dissection,
Did you find the infection?

Explore the root cause of the issue,
If tears come, just grab a tissue.

Reflection,
Redirection,
It's time for resurrection.

Understanding childhood trauma,
Mitigates adult drama.

Affection,
Reconnection,
Let's work together towards perfection.

Let's drown ourselves in education,
To promote effective communication.

September 2020

The Lie

Clouds in the skies.
The truth in disguise.
Guilt in their eyes.
Delayed text replies.

It likes to surprise.
It yells, then it cries.
When confronted, it denies.
While in shock, you surmise.

It seeks compromise.
Restoring soul-ties.
Though it increases in size.
You rescind your good-byes.

Take a word from the wise.
Don't fall under its guise.
The truth never dies.
It will always conquer and rise.

March 11, 2021

Dear Black Queen

Dear black queen, why do you tear me down?
We're in this together,
Both our skin tones are brown.

Dear black queen, why do you act so cold?
I compliment your qualities,
Yet you let mine erode.

Dear black queen, I admire the way you shine,
But my light is bright too,
Can't you admire mine?

Dear black queen, I always give you grace,
But when I make errors,
You spread them with haste.

The world tries to hide us,
The world tries to divide us,
But if we stick together,
The world cannot defy us!

September 2020

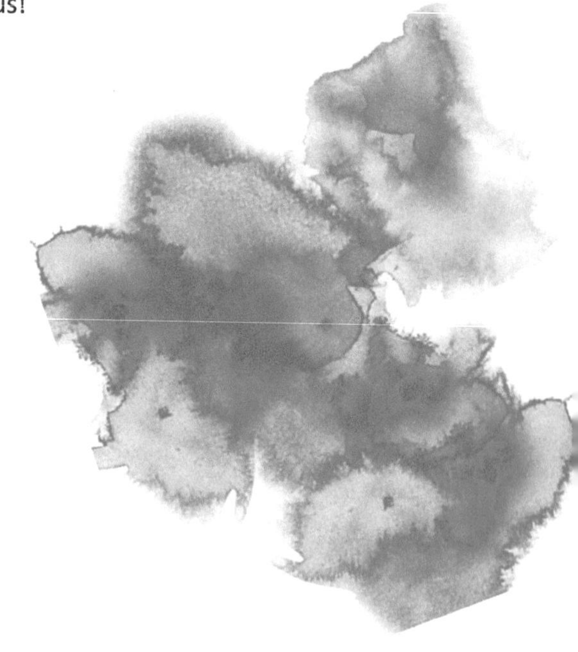

A Child's Anthem

No I don't want to play that game!
Private parts?! Are you insane?!

My body is mine and belongs to me!
There's nothing down there for you to see!

I may be small, but I know my rights!
I will say NO with all my might!

I'll yell and scream at all costs!
I'll bite and scratch to fight you off!

I'll tell someone I love and trust!
I'll do whatever that I must!

I'm a child, don't you know!
These horrible things affect my growth!

I only play games that are G-rated!
And I don't care if we're related!

It's NO to you and anyone else!
I'll do what I can to protect myself!

Don't you dare cause me this pain!
Sexual abuse causes trauma to the brain!

It takes many years for victims to cope!
Many turn to drugs because they've lost hope!

So keep your hands off of me!
Before you catch a felony!

July 2020

Unfit

Unfit for this world,
Why am I here?
My purpose is cloudy,
And very unclear.

Unfit for this world,
Where do I belong?
They want to be right,
I apologize when wrong.

Unfit for this world,
So over this life,
I seek peace,
They seek strife.

Unfit for this world,
I don't get this place,
I speak truth,
They lie to my face,

Unfit for this world,
I want to help the needy,
But unlike some,
They love to be greedy.

Unfit for this world,
Some things are strange,
Unfit for this world,
I must advocate for change.

September 2020

Passive

Wish to die,
Not sure why.

Never attempted,
Never been tempted.

Reached my pinnacle,
Maybe it's chemical.

Is it the anxiety to reach my goal?
Are the weight of my dreams taking a toll?

The longer it takes the more I'm sad,
I want to change the world so freaking bad.

This isn't the world I want to live in,
I want to be where all people win.

No matter the color, ability, or size,
I want to be where there are minimal sighs.

So I guess these feelings will have to stay passive,
Gotta' fulfill these dreams that are so massive.

April 27, 2021

Antes De...(Before)

Before I give you my heart...
Can I count on you if I need you?
Will you do your best to come through?
Will you make me a priority too?

Before I give you my heart...
Will you be selfless and help others?
Will you take time to write me letters?
Will you help me become better?

Before I give you my heart...
Will you take care of me when I get sick?
Will you make tea to help do the trick?
Will your love for me still stick?

Before I give you my heart...
Will you hug me every day?
Will you show love in special ways?
Will you know the right things to say?

Before I give you my heart...
Will you help me if my car breaks down?
Can I expect you to be around?
Can I trust you when you go out of town?

Before I give you my heart...
Will you do your best to quiet my fears?
Will you support me and wipe my tears?
Will your commitment last for infinite years?

Just because I spend time with you,
Doesn't mean you have my heart,
And just because I like you,
Doesn't mean you've got the part.

November 2020

Dear Las Vegas: A Cry for the Homeless

City of lights,
City of might,
But many don't have a place to sleep tonight.

New houses to own,
Even the Raiders have a home,
But so many people are lost and alone.

Vegas, you're the place to be,
A myriad of sights to see,
But what about the homeless plea?

From the Luxor to the Strat,
Your glamour is intact,
But it deters us from what we need to look at.

Vegas, at night you glow,
But there are people beneath the status quo,
People who need your help, you know?

People who fell on difficult times,
People who are victims of violent crimes,
People whose stories should be on Lifetime.

People who never had love and support.
People who were practically raised by the court.
People whose opportunities were cut short.

Cut short by drama,
Cut short by childhood trauma,
Cut short by the convictions of society's dogmas.

Vegas you build, and build and build,
Beauty is the reputation you yield,
But Vegas, sweet Vegas, are you really fulfilled?

Does not your heart cry for the homeless in your streets?
For the people that don't have food to eat?

Vegas you are the City of Lights,
So let's shed some light on basic human rights.

January 2020

Reciprocation

Here's some education,
On the word reciprocation.

It must be hard to master this term.
I think it makes some people squirm.

You can't forget when people are kind.
Don't let their kindness lag behind.

Look for opportunities to bless them back.
This will show your heart is intact.

Listen intently to what they say.
They may give you clues to make their day.

Look for an opportunity to reciprocate.
To let them know you appreciate,

Things they have done for you in the past,
Things they have done without being asked.

It doesn't have to be something grand.
If it comes from the heart, they'll understand.

Without reciprocation things get one-sided,
Most givers get burned out and sometimes they'll hide it.

So next time someone makes you smile,
Put reciprocation back in style.

February 2021

Experiences

I experienced the cold,
So I could offer a coat,
I experienced bad days,
So I could offer a good quote.

I experienced hunger,
So I could offer food,
I experienced sadness,
So I could lift someone's mood.

I experienced lies,
So I could offer the truth,
I experienced innocence,
So I could offer the proof.

I experienced dehydration,
So I could offer a drink,
I experienced losing my thought,
So I could offer time to think.

I experienced a sore throat,
So I could offer tea,
I experienced deceit,
So I could help someone see.

I experienced heartbreak,
So I could offer a song of hope,
I experienced losing a loved one,
So I could help someone cope.

Never doubt your experiences,
They're meant to make you strong,
They're designed to foster empathy,
And help someone else carry on.

June 2021

Absence

Your absence is felt,
My heart tends to melt.

Though you're not present,
Thoughts of you are incessant.

Should I have ended things so abrupt?
Was our time together so corrupt?

Space has given me time to think,
Space provided the missing link.

I enjoyed your love and also your affection,
But was often confused by your subtle rejection.

My feelings left when you broke my trust,
Maybe we just need to focus on us.

Not "us" together, but individually,
Focus on ourselves, do you agree?

I'll miss the fun routine we had,
And how you wiped my tears when I was sad.

I'll miss how you refreshed me when weary,
But I think we need space for us to see clearly.

April 8, 2021

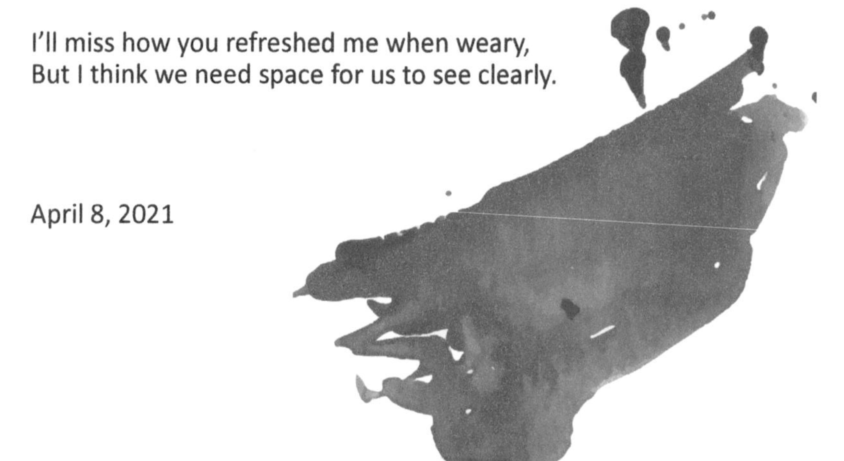

Stability

Stability.
Tranquility.
Agility.
Mobility.

Stability.
Positivity.
Productivity.
Creativity.

Stability.
Sensitivity.
Durability.
Versatility.

Stability.
Flexibility.
Dependability.
Possibilities.

May 2021

Men Should Cry

Men should cry,
You wanna' know why?

My friend named Laura once told me,
Tears are magical, keep reading, you'll see.

A study was conducted to help find out,
The contents of tears and what they're about.

First they took an onion to make someone cry,
And gathered the tears that fell from their eye.

Next they gathered tears from someone stressed,
Perhaps they called the sample, "The Tears of the Distressed."

They studied each sample and the results that they found,
Was nothing short of amazing and actually quite profound.

In the onion induced tears not much was collected,
But in the stressed induced tears, cortisol was detected.

Cortisol? Yes, that's the stress hormone.
It releases in your body when a lot is going on.

So it's important to know when a person cries,
There's more than water that leaves their eyes,

Stress leaves the body and so does pain,
Suppressing those tears would be insane.

Men are taught to be strong and also tough,
But let them cry when they've had enough,

Let them release those feelings of tension,
Perhaps it can mitigate all sorts of contention.

Men are strong, but they're humans too,
So let them relieve stress the way they're designed to.

May 2021
(Newhouse, 2021) and (Brunish, 1957)

Be Humane!

When they're driving you insane,
Be humane!

Even though they've caused you pain,
Be humane!

When your trust starts to wane,
Be humane!

When there's nothing else to gain,
Be humane!

When you're feeling kind of drained,
Be humane!

When your relationship is strained,
Be humane!

Through sunshine and rain,
Be humane!

When they call you out your name,
Be humane!

When your anger is hard to tame,
Be humane!

When you want to complain,
Be humane!

When it doesn't bring you fame,
Be humane!

When your efforts feel in vain,
Be humane!

Though it may seem mundane,
Be humane!

Make this your campaign,
Be humane!

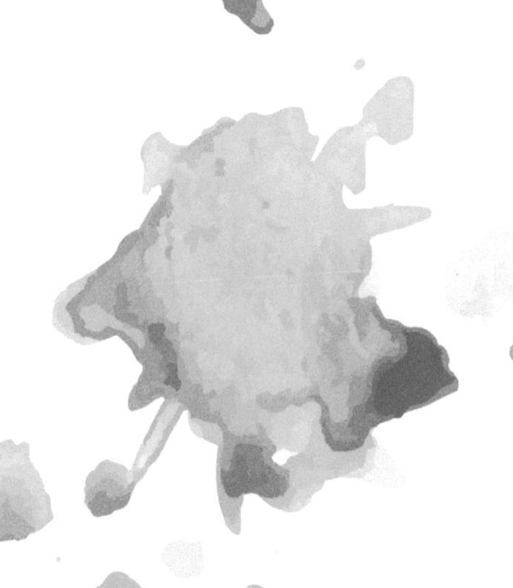

April 19, 2021

"Duncle" Jeff

You were more than my uncle,
You stepped in as my dad,
You were like my best friend,
The best one I had.

You wrote me letters,
Even while at war,
You communicated your love,
Even on foreign shores.

You sent me savings bonds,
Your cards were the best,
You helped purchase my braces,
Now I smile bright with Crest.

I didn't see you much,
You were always at work,
But whenever I got to see you,
It was my biggest perk.

You told me to drink water,
And wear my natural hair,
Even though you were miles away,
It was evident that you cared.

When my money got funny,
You and Auntie bailed me out,
Though you had your own kids,
You were there without a doubt.

I really really miss you,
I cry at random times,
You truly were my favorite,
Our bond was sublime.

I understand why you left me,
But you'll never be replaced,
So in your honor I'll work hard,
To make the world a better place.

May 13, 2021

Empathy

Empathy is going to be the death of me.
I jump in someone else's shoes instantly.

I feel others pain, like it's my very own.
Searching for solutions til' my mind is blown.

I reach in my pockets to help ease their pain.
While most turn their heads and stay in their lane.

I wish I could ignore the stress others feel.
But my compassion overflows; it's hard to conceal.

I love you empathy, but I am worn out.
Perhaps hire more staff to prevent burnout.

We need more people who are willing to care.
We need more people to really be there.

People who don't heap wealth on themselves.
People who bring aid to the bottom shelves.

Empathy, you truly get the best of me.
But I rather have you than luxury.

May 23, 2021

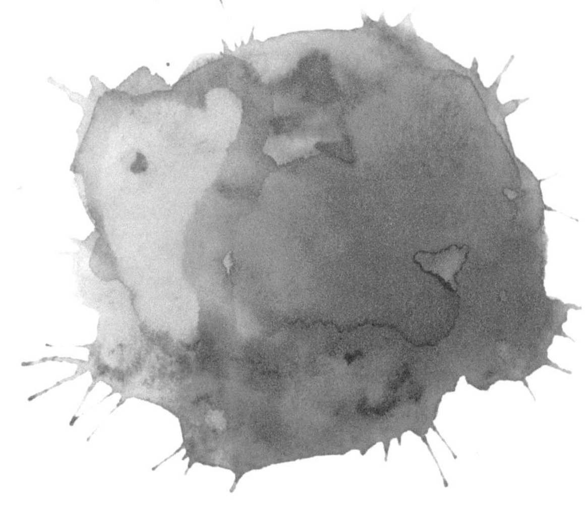

The following poems were written while I was a member of a cult-like entity that operated and still operates like a church. While in this emotionally toxic and abusive place, there was a young man that became my best friend and crush in a matter of five weeks. That crush lasted for about 8 years. Crazy! I know! These poems display my feelings for him then and my feelings for the "church" leadership now. For more information on my disillusioned experience please scan the QR code below with your camera phone to access my YouTube channel. You may type the link in your browser as well. Viewer discretion advised. Just kidding! LOL!

https://youtu.be/GQ-hCIzIeFI

Heart Transplant

Thump...you...thump...you,
This is what my heart tends to do.

It reflects on your words, your love, and your face,
It reminisces on your warm and cuddly embrace.

How often does this occur, one might ask?
More than the memories of an enjoyable past.

Ever since 19, that's when you entered in,
It was something very random and all of a sudden.

These feelings weren't invited; they sort of just came,
But now my heart constantly recites your name.

I try to conceal it as best as I can,
But deep down inside, I'm your number one fan.

I admit to these feelings because I'm the owner,
But I think I need a transplant; Do you know any donors?

You bring my heart so much cheer,
But the way you feel, isn't quite clear.

So a heart transplant is my goal and quest,
I must put these feelings that I have to rest.

February 14, 2012

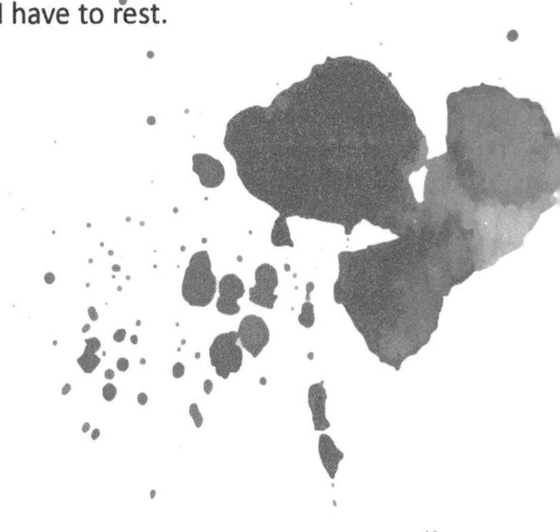

Fading

It feels like I'm fading.

Fading from everything I've ever known,
Fading from things I've called my own.

Fading away from people I loved,
Fading away like a frightened dove.

Don't know whether to go east or west,
I just want God to put this mind to rest.

Constant battles rise within me,
Rather than consent, I always disagree.

Looking for answers through fasting and prayer,
Constantly yelling, "Can you hear me up there?!"

Why is stuff confusing? Where's the yay and nay?
These are the constant things that I pray.

Isn't the Bible supposed to be clear?
I want this confusion to disappear.

Nothing makes sense; everything is opaque.
I really feel like my soul is at stake.

February 2012

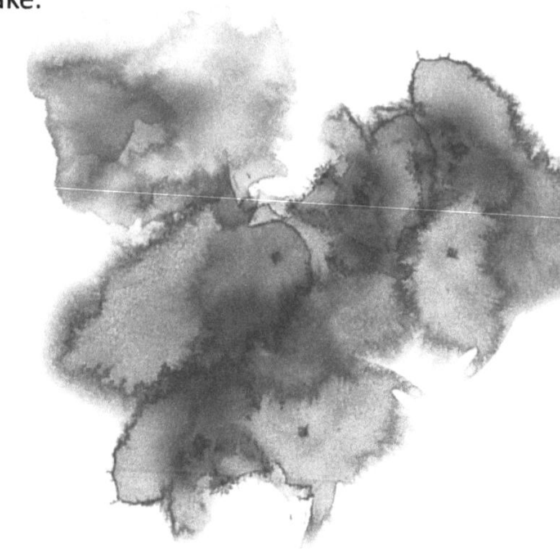

The Split

So I finally did it.
I let you go.
2 months since the split,
And residual feelings still show.

Still craving the attention,
The feeling of being liked,
And let's not forget to mention,
Those hugs were just right.

But now I stand alone.
Not a friend in view.
There's not much use of my phone,
Cause' I can't talk to you.

I saw the idolatry.
No doubt it was there.
In my dreams resided your imagery.
It was more than I could bear.

So I had to let you go,
And spiritually pick up the pace,
Though your eyes still have that glow,
I had to get back in God's face.

April 26, 2012

Free!

At first I was mad at you,
But now I understand,
We were both just lonely,
It was a part of the devil's plan.

He wanted to distract us,
Steer us away from God's path,
He wanted to deter us,
Smack dab into God's wrath.

At first I thought you played me,
A jerk you were indeed,
But then I came to see,
We were just fulfilling a need.

A need to be cherished,
And a need to be loved,
A need to be thought of,
And a need to be hugged.

But through my conviction,
And as the Lord began to wean,
He revealed a powerful scripture,
Psalm 145:16.

He will satisfy our desires,
Every one we have,
But we have to give Him our whole heart,
We can't just give Him half.

May 3, 2012

Love Unprecedented

I'm in love with the idea of being loved,
To be adored, cherished, and even thought of.

To invade someone's thoughts at random times,
To be written about in a poem that rhymes.

To be loved so much, it's impossible to lie,
To be a favorite hello and a hardest good-bye.

To be the motivation to wake up and pray,
To be the cause of a smile during the workday.

May 2012

Just Because...

Thoughts of you interrupt my day,
I miss you the moment you walk away.

I admire all of the things you do,
It's always a joy spending time with you.

Today isn't a holiday, or special occasion,
You are the epitome of my persuasion.

May 2012

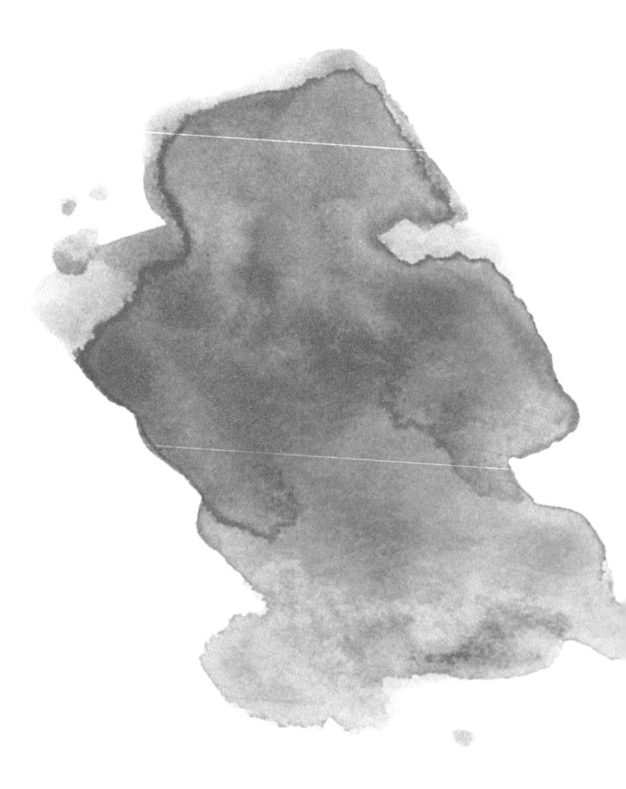

The Sabbatical

To disappear is what I'd rather do,
Than to still be in love with you.

It makes no sense that I still care,
When emotionally, you're not even there.

To cut all communication, was my goal,
But in my script, you still play a role.

I thought there was a need for this sabbatical,
But I'm starting to think it's impractical.

You're all I tend to think about,
It's so frustrating, I want to shout!

I've never felt this way before,
When we talked all night, I still wanted more.

In the mornings, I looked forward to you,
A text or an email would always come through.

But my feelings were getting a little obsessive,
And thoughts of you were getting excessive.

So I said I'm taking a break this year,
But now I just seem to wipe my tears.

I miss the validations,
I miss the congratulations.

I want to talk to you badly,
I guess I'm in love with you, madly.

February 21, 2013

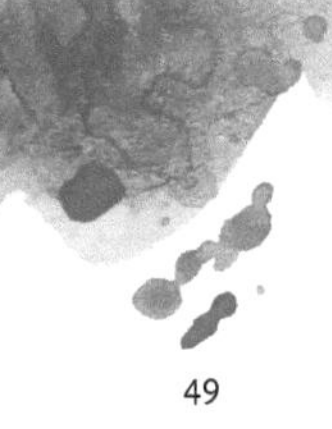

The Fling

You have no idea how I feel right now,
My state of mind is simply at WOW.

But as I'm willfully writing this,
I'm telling my feelings, "Case dismissed!"

It shouldn't be hard, cuz' I knew from the start,
I never really made it, inside your heart.

Maybe on the brink, but not fully in,
You stayed in shallow waters, while I was in the deep end.

Though you lavished me with gifts and tons of attention,
I knew I wouldn't remain in your heart's retention.

But today I'm letting you go,
Well...at least I think so.

I don't like the way my days are going,
You enter my thoughts without me knowing,

I check my phone awaiting your message,
If I counted the times, it would be excessive.

You are what I seemed to look forward to,
I didn't despise my life when I was with you.

But now as I look at everything,
Our time was temporal; It was only a fling.

I must've been crazy to think we'd ever be,
The thought is so wild; Someone should admit me.

So I'm letting you go; Please don't ever come back,
Cuz' this "re-getting" over you process is really wack.

Thank you for our short period of unrestrained pursuit,
Please excuse me, I think I need a system reboot.

February 14, 2014

Shoulda'

Shoulda' told my heart no,
When it wanted to love you.
Shoulda' told my heart no,
When it wanted to hold you.

Shoulda' told my heart no,
But yes felt good.
Shoulda' told my heart no,
If I could go back, I would.

Shoulda' told my heart no,
Cuz' now you're not here.
Shoulda told my heart no,
Now I just wipe my tears.

Shoulda' told my heart no,
Thought we'd be friends forever.
Shoulda' told my heart no,
Now you're just lost treasure.

December 2015

Tithes

"Pay your tithes,"
That's a bunch of lies,
How dare you guys,
You're crooks in disguise.

"Sow a seed,"
"It's a really good deed,"
Baby please,
It's fueling your greed.

"Give first fruits,"
I'd like to refute,
The money is for you,
Your Bentley is proof.

"Give 10 percent,"
That doesn't make sense,
If I give my cent,
Who will pay my rent?

January 2021

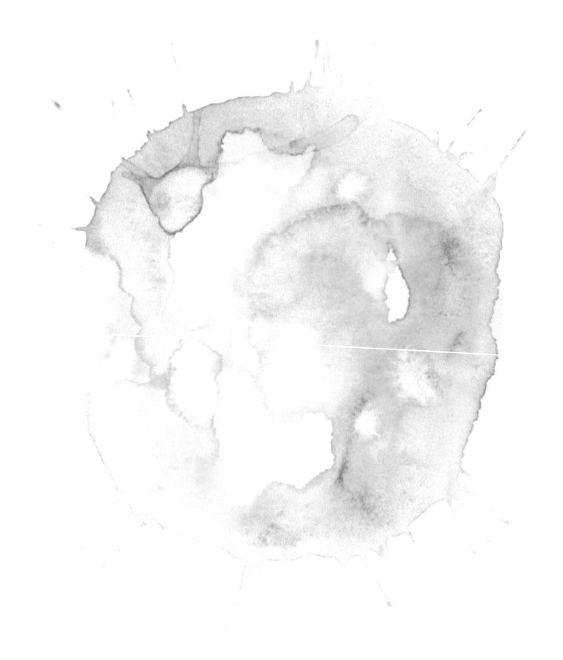

"Leader Astrayer"

I was your spiritual daughter for 22 years,
Your prolific speech always brought me to tears.

Within those years we talked 3 times,
The third conversation made me resign.

Resign from your lies and your deceit,
Resign from your willingness to be false and cheat.

My heart sank when I saw your face,
The day I decided to create some space.

Space between you and all your lies,
Space from your ability to cover my eyes.

I had my doubts, but not about you,
I always believed, your words were true.

But just like the serpent, you beguiled me,
Just so you could fulfill your fantasy.

Just so you could have a million-dollar home,
While your church members are stuck in Stockholm.

I really don't know how you sleep at night,
But therapy has given me insight.

You made a mistake, but didn't want to let go,
It all makes sense, trust me I know.

But lying about miracles is out of line,
I can't believe I didn't see all the signs.

Auditory hallucinations are very real,
Maybe see a therapist so you can heal.

Don't take offense, I'm not throwing shade,
I'm just "following" you and trying to get paid.

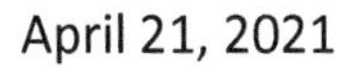

April 21, 2021

Last Lady

No longer are you first in my book,
All your teachings I've forsook.

I'm ashamed of your selfish ways,
Is this how you'll end your days?

I fell for all your wicked lies,
You preached about God in disguise.

You told us to serve you and God would be pleased,
You told us to pray and spend hours on our knees.

I get sick to my stomach just thinking of you,
How long will this madness continue?

You've caused so much stress and so much pain,
How much more do you need to gain?

You've played this game for many years,
You've watch people suffer and wipe their tears.

People have died, believing in you,
But your only concern is the revenue.

Someone must put a stop to this,
If I don't speak up, I'll be remiss.

I'll stand against you with all bravery,
To help others escape from this slavery.

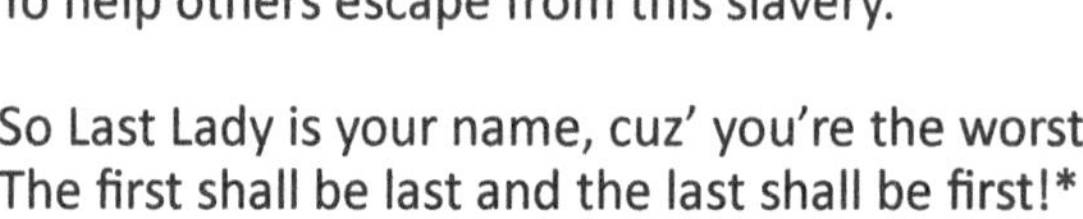

So Last Lady is your name, cuz' you're the worst,
The first shall be last and the last shall be first!*

April 2021
*paraphrased Holy Bible scripture from Matthew 20:16

Prima Donna

You have not the slightest clue,
How much I looked up to you.

I admired the way you combed your hair,
No one's wet set could compare.

I admired how you visited the sick,
And how you wrote plays that were epic.

But over the years I noticed you lied,
And you often were the reason why I cried.

You ignored my texts one by one,
And being left out, wasn't much fun.

I was crippled by fear and anxiety,
Ruminating thoughts, thinking God was mad at me.

The selfishness you possess is beyond comprehension,
Interacting with you almost caused hypertension.

I can't believe I wasted all this time,
You took so much space on my life's timeline.

I don't really blame you, cuz' you were raised this way,
You're not fully responsible for your parents' foul play.

It's not your fault that they conceal the truth,
It's not your fault that they hide the proof.

I still think you have a good heart,
Even though you played a major part.

A part in financial and emotional abuse,
A major part that I cannot excuse.

And though you may look at me strange,
There's still some time for you to change.

March 2021

Dear Louis V. (pronounced Louie)

Dear Louis V.,
I wish I could've met you.
The church is corrupt,
Not all of them, just a few.

Dear Louis V.,
I think the church is cursed.
Last Lady's sell their souls,
Just for your purse.

Dear Louis V.,
Can you come back?
Tell them to help others,
And give to those who lack.

Dear Louis V.,
You really need to come.
Your bags are nice,
But their hearts are numb.

They only care about controlling people.
They hide their dirt behind the steeple.

They lie, lie, lie, to get ahead,
And use you to feel better, even though you're dead.

Instead of addressing their low self-esteem,
They buy your clothes to feel supreme.

Louis V. you are crippling the church.
All because they love your fashion and "merch".

I don't know what else to do,
The church doesn't look the way it used to.

While the church members are praying for their needs,
The "first fam" is rocking Louis V.

April 21, 2021

Let God's People Go!

Let God's people go!
Let God's people know!

Tell them that you lied!
Tell them! Drop your pride!

Tell them that you're phony!
Tell them it's all bologna!

Step down from your throne!
Leave God's people alone!

You already have your wealth!
You already have your health!

Stop playing with their heads!
Stop before I call the Feds!

March 2021

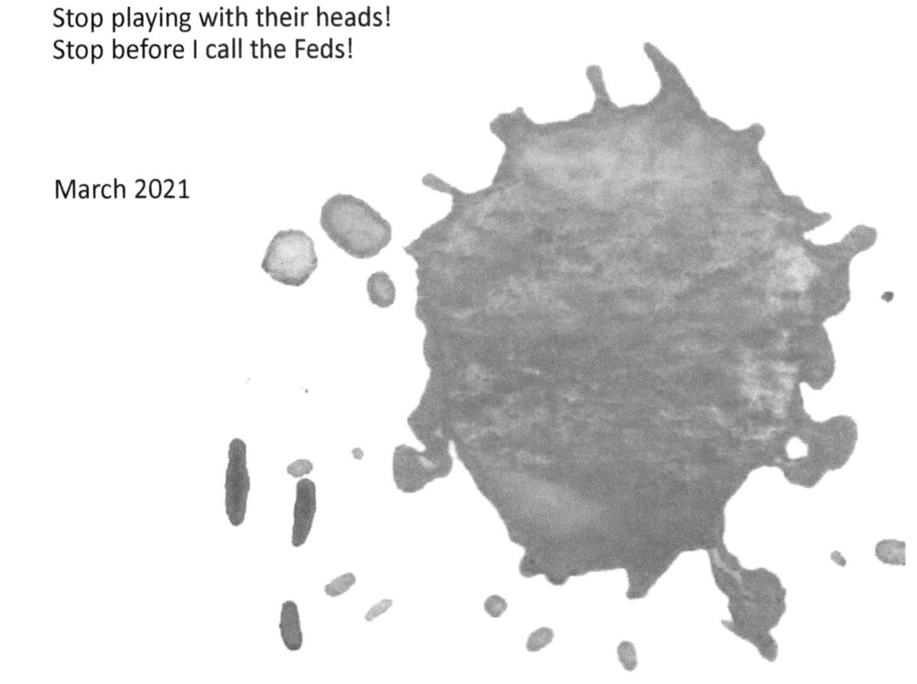

Restitution

I want restitution,
For all my contributions.

I want every dime,
For every ounce of my time.

I paid for lies,
In the form of tithes.

I want what's mine,
I'm next in line.

Not for a miracle, but for a refund,
Perhaps I can have it from a trust fund?

Please don't confuse my motive or intent,
I just need a reimbursement.

April 2021

REFERENCES

Brunish, R. (1957). The Protein Components of Human Tears. Archives of Ophthalmology,57(4), 554-556. doi:10.1001/archopht.1957.00930050566009

Jakes, T. (2015, September 13). Called. Speech presented at The Potter's House in Texas, Dallas. Retrieved from https://youtu.be/5hTAOUtIomU (Clip time 5:52-6:35)

Newhouse, L. (2021, March 01). Is crying good for you? Retrieved May 22, 2021, from https://www.health.harvard.edu/blog/is-crying-good-for-you-2021030122020

SPLATTER ART CREDITS

01 @[VASABII] VIA CANVA.COM

03 @[ONEWHYSTUDIO] VIA CANVA.COM

07 @[ARTNERDLUXE] VIA CANVA.COM
@[KREATIVSPACE] VIA CANVA.COM

09 @[GOJA1 FROM GETTY IMAGES PRO] VIA CANVA.COM

11 @[GOJA1 FROM GETTY IMAGES PRO] VIA CANVA.COM

13 @[KHANEEROS] VIA CANVA.COM

15 @[KHANEEROS] VIA CANVA.COM
16 @[KHANEEROS] VIA CANVA.COM
17 @[KHANEEROS] VIA CANVA.COM

18 @[ONEWHYSTUDIO] VIA CANVA.COM
19 @[ONEWHYSTUDIO] VIA CANVA.COM
20 @[ONEWHYSTUDIO] VIA CANVA.COM
21 @[ONEWHYSTUDIO] VIA CANVA.COM
22 @[ONEWHYSTUDIO] VIA CANVA.COM

23 @[DIGITAL SILK] VIA CANVA.COM

24 @[ONEWHYSTUDIO] VIA CANVA.COM

25 @[SKETCHIFY] VIA CANVA.COM

26 @[#VALOURINE'S IMAGES] VIA CANVA.COM

27 @[DIGITAL SILK] VIA CANVA.COM

SPLATTER ART CREDITS

28 @[ALLIES INTERACTIVE] VIA CANVA.COM

29 @[WATERCOLOREPSTUDIO] VIA CANVA.COM

30 @[#VALOURINE'S IMAGES] VIA CANVA.COM

31 @[DIGITAL SILK] VIA CANVA.COM

32 @[DIGITAL SILK] VIA CANVA.COM

33 @[AIDENOPOLY] VIA CANVA.COM

34 @[VASABII] VIA CANVA.COM

35 @[ANKADROZD] VIA CANVA.COM

36 @[VASABII] VIA CANVA.COM(FRONT COVER ALSO)

37 @[VASABII] VIA CANVA.COM(FRONT COVER ALSO)

38 @[ONEWHYSTUDIO] VIA CANVA.COM

39 @[DIGITAL SILK] VIA CANVA.COM

41 @[LEREMY GAN] VIA CANVA.COM
@[MOONNOON] VIA CANVA.COM
@[MARKETPLACE DESIGNERS] VIA CANVA.COM

SPLATTER ART CREDITS

43 @[VASABII] VIA CANVA.COM(FRONT COVER ALSO)
@[LEREMY GAN] VIA CANVA.COM (LOGO)

44 @[#VALOURINE'S IMAGES] VIA CANVA.COM
@[LEREMY GAN] VIA CANVA.COM (LOGO)

45 @[JEMASTOCK2] VIA CANVA.COM (FRONT COVER ALSO)
@[LEREMY GAN] VIA CANVA.COM (LOGO)

46 @[SKETCHIFY] VIA CANVA.COM
@[LEREMY GAN] VIA CANVA.COM (LOGO)

47 @[DIGITAL SILK] VIA CANVA.COM
@[LEREMY GAN] VIA CANVA.COM (LOGO)

48 @[SKETCHIFY] VIA CANVA.COM
@[LEREMY GAN] VIA CANVA.COM (LOGO)

49 @[AKHMAD REZA FAUZI] VIA CANVA.COM
@[LEREMY GAN] VIA CANVA.COM (LOGO)

50 @[AIDENOPOLY] VIA CANVA.COM
@[LEREMY GAN] VIA CANVA.COM (LOGO)

SPLATTER ART CREDITS

51 @[DIGITAL SILK] VIA CANVA.COM
@[LEREMY GAN] VIA CANVA.COM
(LOGO)

52 @[DIGITAL SILK] VIA CANVA.COM
@[LEREMY GAN] VIA CANVA.COM
(LOGO)

53 @[VASABII] VIA CANVA.COM
@[LEREMY GAN] VIA CANVA.COM
(LOGO)

54 @[VASABII] VIA CANVA.COM
@[LEREMY GAN] VIA CANVA.COM
(LOGO)

55 @[KRISTY PARGETER] VIA CANVA.COM (COVER)
@[LEREMY GAN] VIA CANVA.COM
(LOGO)

56 @[WATERCOLOREPSTUDIO] VIA CANVA.COM
@[LEREMY GAN] VIA CANVA.COM
(LOGO)

57 @[WATERCOLOREPSTUDIO] VIA CANVA.COM
@[LEREMY GAN] VIA CANVA.COM
(LOGO)

58 @[KSANIA DESIGNER] VIA CANVA.COM
@[LEREMY GAN] VIA CANVA.COM
(LOGO)

59 @[KHANEEROS] VIA CANVA.COM
@[LEREMY GAN] VIA CANVA.COM
(LOGO)

SPLATTER ART CREDITS

65 @[DKDESIGNZ] VIA CANVA.COM
@[SPARKLESTROKE GLOBAL] VIA CANVA.COM (FRONT/BACK COVER & TITLE PAGE)
@[KRISTY PARGETER] VIA CANVA.COM (TITLE & DEDICATION PAGE ALSO)
@[VASABII] VIA CANVA.COM (TITLE & DEDICATION PAGE ALSO)
@[VASABII] VIA CANVA.COM (TITLE & DEDICATION PAGE ALSO)
@[JEMASTOCK2] VIA CANVA.COM (TITLE & DEDICATION PAGE ALSO)
@[VASABII] VIA CANVA.COM (TITLE & DEDICATION PAGE ALSO)

67 @[LEREMY GAN] VIA CANVA.COM
@[MARKETPLACE DESIGNERS] VIA CANVA.COM

68 @[LANASHAMART] VIA CANVA.COM

"Sometimes life feels like spilled paint, but when it spills on a canvas, it's art."

-Simone C. Phillips

For more information regarding my cult-like experience, scan the QR code using your camera phone or type the link in your browser below!

https://youtu.be/GQ-hCIzIeFI

If you enjoyed this book and would like to contact Simone, feel free to reach her via email at disillusionedchurchgirl@gmail.com. She would love to hear from you.

Thank you so much for purchasing my book! If you would like to purchase more copies please scan the QR code below with your camera phone or visit http:www.writersrepublic.com/bookshop/splatters-heart.
You may also place orders via phone by calling 1-877-656-6838.

CPSIA information can be obtained
at www.ICGtesting.com
Printed in the USA
BVHW091047231121
622346BV00001B/5